# WHY DO WE SAY THAT?

101 Idioms, Phrases, Sayings & Facts! A Brief History On
Where They Come From!

SCOTT MATTHEWS

*The more that you read, the more things you will know. The more you learn, the more places you'll go. - Dr. Seuss*

# Contents

# Introduction

Are you ready to explore the intriguing world of idioms? You might be surprised to learn that we use them daily, sometimes without even realizing it! But have you ever wondered about the origins of these fascinating phrases?

Also called idiomatic expressions, idioms have slowly been introduced into the English language as it has developed over time. These expressions have a commonly understood meaning which varies from the literal meaning of the words being spoken, read, or written.

As we explore the origins of idioms, we'll be taking a journey back in time to discover what the English-speaking world was like when these phrases were first used. While some idioms have clear origins, others have evolved over time, passed down through oral tradition, and may have unknown origins or multiple theories of where they came from. Despite this, the enduring popularity and widespread use of these idioms continue to pique our interest and inspire further inquiry.

So let's dive right into the wonderful world of idioms and where they come from!

# 1. Behind the scenes

The idiom "behind the scenes" has its roots in theater. It originally referred to the area behind the stage where actors and crew prepare for a performance. The colloquial phrase has been used since at least the early 19th century to refer to actions or activities that take place out of public view. The phrase has a metaphorical meaning, referring to the unseen work that goes into creating something or making something happen.

## 2. Keep your eyes peeled

There are two origin stories linked to this idiom. Firstly, when someone peels an orange, they remove its skin and open it up. So to "keep your eyes peeled" means keeping the skin, or eyelids, off your eyes, ensuring that they are open. The second origin story goes back to the founding of the Metropolitan Police Force in London in 1829. Sir Robert Peel, the Home Secretary at the time, founded the force, and policemen were quickly nicknamed 'bobbies' or 'peelers,' both derived from his name. Peelers kept watch on unsavory characters, and while the nickname has faded into obscurity, the idiom lives on. Today, to "keep your eyes peeled" is used more broadly to mean to be on the lookout or pay close attention to something, particularly to be ready for any potential challenges or opportunities. It is often used to express a sense of vigilance or alertness and the need to be prepared for whatever may come.

## 3. Builder's tea

The term "builder's tea" is a British phrase that refers to a type of tea that is typically consumed by manual laborers, particularly construction workers. The tea is typically made with strong black tea leaves and is served with milk and sugar. It is also known as "builder's brew" or "working man's tea." The phrase originated in the 20th century, when tea consumption was widespread among the working class population, especially among those who were working in manual labor jobs such as construction. Nowadays, it might simply refer to a strong cup of tea.

## 4. Separate the wheat from the chaff

The phrase "separate the wheat from the chaff" means to set apart valuable or useful things from less valuable or useful ones. This saying originates from the agricultural practice of separating the wheat kernels from the inedible chaff (the dry, scaly protective coverings of cereal grain) using a process called winnowing. This was done by throwing the mixture of wheat and chaff into the air on a windy day, and the chaff would blow away while the heavier wheat kernels would fall back to the ground. It has its origins in the Bible as a metaphor that speaks about how God will separate those who are worthy and those who are unworthy. In the Bible, it is written, "His winnowing fork is in his hand, and he will clear his threshing floor, gathering his wheat into the barn and burning up the chaff with unquenchable fire." This metaphor was used to explain how the good will be rewarded and the bad will be punished. In modern times, it might refer to a sport where the upper echelon is clearly better than the rest.

# 5. Cool as a cucumber

The idiom "cool as a cucumber" is used to describe someone who remains calm and composed during difficult or stressful situations. It originated in the early 18th century, likely from the physical properties of cucumbers which have a cool and refreshing temperature when cut open due to their high water content (which can be as high as 96%). The term is often used to describe someone level-headed and able to maintain composure in the face of adversity. The original meaning of the word "cool" in the phrase referred to self-confident and calm, which was first written in a verse by British poet John Gay in his 1732 poem *New Song on New Similies*: "Cool as a cucumber could see the rest of womankind."

## 6. Egg on your face

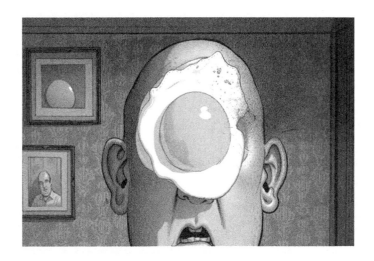

The idiom "egg on your face" is a colloquial expression that denotes being embarrassed or humiliated, often as a result of one's own actions or words. The origin of this American idiom is unknown. One possible source of the phrase can be traced back to popular theater during the 1800s and early 1900s, where sub-par actors would often be pelted with rotten vegetables and eggs, resulting in them having egg on their faces. Another possible origin stems from the farmyard, where farm dogs sometimes develop a taste for eggs. To identify the culprit, a farmer may look for the egg on the dog's face as a sign of guilt. The metaphor suggests that one is embarrassed or humiliated, much like an actor might feel embarrassed if they had egg on their face, or a dog might feel guilty if it had egg on its face. The earliest written record of this phrase dates back to the early 20th century, in a book called *The American Language* by H.L. Mencken, published in 1919, where it is defined as "to be embarrassed or humiliated, often as a result of one's own actions or words."

# 7. Sit tight

The phrase "to sit tight" means to remain in a passive or inactive position and wait for something to happen, rather than taking action. It can also mean to remain in a particular situation, often a difficult or challenging one, and not make any changes. It is often used to suggest that someone should not act impulsively or take unnecessary risks, but instead wait for a more favorable outcome. The term originated in the early 20th century, and was used in the context of stock market investments, suggesting that investors should not panic and sell their stocks during a market downturn, but instead hold on to them and wait for the market to recover.

## 8. Cry over spilled milk

The idiom "cry over spilled milk" is an expression that means to complain or grieve over something that has already happened and cannot be changed. The origin of the phrase comes from the fact that crying over spilled milk is considered a pointless and futile action, as the milk is already spilled and cannot be recovered, and is often prefaced with "there's no use crying over spilled milk." The phrase was first seen in 1659 by writer and historian James Howell in one of his works, *Paramoigraphy*.

## 9. Neck and neck

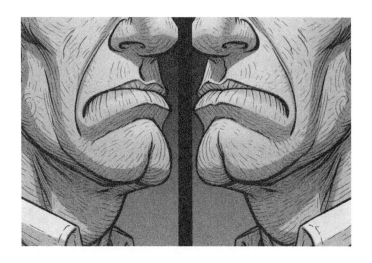

The idiom "neck and neck" has its roots in horse racing. The phrase was first recorded in the early 1800s and was used to describe a close race where the winning horse "won by a neck." This is because during a tight race, what is often observed are the horses running side by side, with their necks stretched out as they compete to be the first to cross the finish line. Thus, the commentator is often heard saying "they were neck and neck, but the distance between the winning horse and the second horse was a neck."

## 10. Wild goose chase

The term "wild goose chase" refers to a futile or pointless pursuit or search. It is often used to describe a situation in which someone is trying to achieve or find something that is unlikely to be successful. The origins of this idiom can be traced back to the 16th century, when it was used to describe a type of horse race in which riders followed a leader, who was often depicted as a goose. The leader would lead the riders on a serpentine route, and the riders would follow as closely as possible. The phrase "wild goose chase" was first recorded in this context in the book *The Art of Horsemanship* by the English poet Gervase Markham, which was published in 1593. The idiom is also mentioned in the play *Romeo and Juliet* by William Shakespeare. In Act 2, Scene 4, the character Mercutio uses the phrase to describe the pursuit of a woman. He says, "Nay, if our wits run the wild-goose chase, I am done; for thou hast more of the wild goose in one of thy wits than, I am sure, I have in my whole five."

# Did You Know?

You might notice that a lot of idioms are derived from gambling. This is because gambling has been a popular pastime for centuries and has played an important role in many cultures. In the past, gambling was not just a form of entertainment but also a way to make a living.

Gambling is often associated with risk and uncertainty, and many idioms that come from gambling reflect this. For example, "to bet on a long shot" means to take a risk on something unlikely to happen, while "to hedge your bets" means to protect yourself from potential losses by making multiple bets.

Additionally, gambling often involves using metaphors related to money, such as "ante up," meaning to put money in the pot, and "to cash in" meaning to take your winnings. Gambling also often involves expressions of chance and luck, such as "to roll the dice," meaning to take a chance, or "to play your cards right," meaning to make the best of the situation.

Gambling also has a long history of being a social activity and, in many cases, idioms that come from gambling reflect this aspect. Gambling idioms are often used in the context of making a decision or taking a risk or making a bet, which is why they are often used in everyday life beyond the gambling context. Some of the oldest games dating back to ancient times:

1. Dice games: Dice games have been around since ancient times, with evidence of dice usage dating back to 6000 BC. Dice games were popular among the

ancient Greeks, Romans, and Egyptians. These games involved rolling dice to determine the outcome and were played for both entertainment and financial gain.

2. Keno: Keno is a Chinese lottery game that dates back to around 200 BC. The game involves picking numbers and betting on the outcome of a drawing, much like modern-day lottery games. Keno was used as a way to raise funds for the state and it remains a popular form of gambling in many countries.

3. Chaupar/Pachisi: Chaupar, also known as Pachisi, is a board game from ancient India that is considered a precursor to modern-day parcheesi. The game involves moving pieces around a board based on the roll of dice, and was played by Indian royalty. It was considered a symbol of wealth and status.

4. Hnefatafl: Hnefatafl is a Scandinavian board game from the Viking Age that was played for both entertainment and gambling purposes. The game involves moving pieces on a board to capture the opponent's king and was played by both common people and royalty.

5. Hazard: Hazard is an English game of chance that was played with dice and is considered one of the earliest forms of the modern day game of craps. The game involved betting on the outcome of dice rolls and was played by royalty and commoners alike. Hazard was introduced to the American colonies and became popular in the United States, where it evolved into the game of craps that is played today.

6. Chess: Chess has been played for over a thousand years by people of all social classes and was considered a symbol of intelligence and strategy.

## 11. The apple of one's eye

The idiom "the apple of one's eye" is used to describe someone who is greatly valued or cherished. The phrase originates from the Bible, specifically in Deuteronomy 32:10 where it is written, "He found him in a desert land, and in the waste howling wilderness; he led him about, he instructed him, he kept him as the apple of his eye." This phrase is a metaphor that compares someone to the pupil of the eye, which is considered precious and protected. Often, "the apple of one's eye" refers to a loved one whom the speaker values above all others.

## 12. Pigeonhole

The term "pigeonhole" has a rich history dating back to the late 1500s, where it was originally used to describe a small recess for pigeons to nest in. This bird box-like shape can still be seen in modern units today. During medieval times, farmers and those in the agriculture trade commonly utilized pigeonholes to keep domestic birds for their families' consumption, which were also referred to as dovecotes and closely resembled tiny houses for birds to nest in. In the late 1700s, the term "pigeonhole" was adopted to describe office furniture used for housing and organizing paperwork, due to their close resemblance to the domestic pigeonholes. Today, pigeonholes are still widely used in schools and businesses around the world, particularly in mailrooms as they greatly improve the organization of mail that needs to be manually sorted.

# 13. On the line

The idiom "on the line" refers to something that is at risk, often in a high-pressure or high-stakes situation. Some sources suggest that the term may have originated as early as the end of the 17th century, while others suggest that it may have originated as late as the 1940s. It is possible that the phrase has evolved over time and has been used in a variety of different contexts, including aboard British naval vessels, in gambling dens, and to describe urgency in a tense situation.

## 14. Hit the nail on the head

"Hit the nail on the head" is a common saying that refers to the precise identification or core essence of something. Additionally, it may also connote the successful resolution of a problem or the provision of a correct solution. The phrase is derived from carpentry, where the analogy is straightforward: when hammering in a nail, striking the head is crucial and failure to do so may result in damage to the surface or even injury. In casual conversation, a person might express something in a way that resonates with you or perfectly encapsulates a point, and you could rightly say that they "hit the nail on the head."

## 15. Your guess is as good as mine

"Your guess is as good as mine" refers to a situation in which someone does not have any more information or knowledge than the other person. It originated in the 19th century and is derived from the idea of making an educated guess or estimation about something based on the available information. Today, the phrase is used to convey a sense of uncertainty or lack of knowledge.

## 16. We're not in Kansas anymore

The saying "we're not in Kansas anymore" is used to describe a situation in which someone is in a very different place or circumstances than they are used to. It is often used to describe a person who has left their familiar surroundings and is now in a new or unfamiliar environment. The phrase "we're not in Kansas anymore" is a reference to the 1939 film *The Wizard of Oz*, in which the main character, Dorothy, is transported from her home in Kansas to the fantastical land of Oz. In the film, Dorothy repeatedly says "we're not in Kansas anymore" as a way of expressing her surprise and disorientation as she travels the land and meets all sorts of strange people and creatures.

## 17. Up a creek without a paddle

The idiom "up a creek without a paddle" refers to a situation in which someone is in a difficult or problematic position and lacks the means or resources to extricate themselves. It originated in the 19th century and is derived from the idea of being in a small boat or canoe without a paddle, which would make it difficult or impossible to steer or move the boat. Today, the phrase is used to convey a sense of helplessness or perhaps to note that the person in the predicament should have been better prepared.

## 18. Dead end job

A "dead end job" is commonly used to describe employment that has limited or no potential for advancement or professional growth. These types of jobs are often characterized by low wages and unsatisfying work that does not provide a clear trajectory for career development or fulfillment for the employee. The expression has its origins in the early 20th century, and is thought to have been derived from the term "dead end," which was first used in the 1880s to describe a blocked water pipe. By the 1920s, it had evolved into an idiom meaning a situation with no way out.

## 19. Up in the air

The idiom "up in the air" is used to describe a situation that is uncertain, unresolved, or in a state of flux. The term is often used when a plan hasn't been settled on or where there is a lack of clarity or certainty about an outcome from an endeavor. The phrase "up in the air" has been in use since the early 20th century, and it most likely originated from the literal meaning of something being in the air, such as an airplane or a balloon. In the early 20th century, airplanes were new technology, and the idea of something being "up in the air" was associated with the uncertainty and unpredictability of flight. It is also possible that the phrase has origins in nautical terminology, where ships at anchor in a port, ready for departure and with sails opened, are said to be "up in the air."

## 20. Look before you leap

The idea that one should "look before you leap" refers to the importance of considering the potential consequences of one's actions before making a decision or taking the first step. It is thought to have originated in the 16th century and is likely derived from the idea of looking before jumping to avoid danger. It can be used to describe a wide range of situations, from casual conversation to life-changing decisions. Today, the phrase is often used to convey a sense of caution or prudence, where another person might warn you to "look before you leap" into a fraught situation.

# Did You Know?

Many idioms come from famous poets, philosophers, and writers from the past. This is because they were some of the most well-known and respected figures of their time, and their words and phrases were widely read and shared. They often wrote about the human experience and used vivid and imaginative language to convey their ideas. These phrases and expressions were used by the general population, and over time they became a part of everyday language and culture. Additionally, literature and poetry were more prevalent in the past and people were more likely to be exposed to them, which also played a role in idioms becoming a part of everyday language. Furthermore, many of these writers were trying to convey complex ideas in simple ways, which made their language and phrases more memorable and useful for everyday use.

Some famous poets, philosophers, and writers who have contributed idioms to the English language include:

William Shakespeare: Shakespeare is widely considered one of the greatest writers in the English language and many of his plays and poems are still widely read and performed today. Many idioms and phrases that we use nowadays come from his works, such as "to be or not to be," "the world is your oyster," and "good riddance."

George Orwell: George Orwell is best known for his books *1984* and *Animal Farm*. Phrases like "big brother" and "doublethink" originated from his book *1984*.

Benjamin Franklin: Benjamin Franklin was a statesman, scientist, and writer, and is known for his famous idioms like "a penny saved is a penny earned."

Confucius: Confucius is a Chinese philosopher, his teachings and sayings have been widely known and used, idioms like "Confucius say."

Mark Twain: Mark Twain, an American writer and humorist, is known for his famous idioms like "the truth is stranger than fiction."

Socrates: Socrates is considered one of the founders of Western philosophy. The phrase "the Socratic method" refers to a method of teaching and learning through asking questions and engaging in dialogue.

Aristotle: Aristotle was a student of Plato and tutored Alexander the Great, he wrote on various subjects including his book *Rhetoric*, and his name is associated with terms like "Aristotelian logic" and "Aristotelian syllogism."

Plato: Plato was a student of Socrates and a teacher of Aristotle, he wrote many *Dialogues*, and some of the most famous idioms that come from Plato's works include "Platonic love" and "Plato's cave."

## 21. Whet one's appetite

The phrase "whet one's appetite" means to stimulate or increase interest in something. It is often used with a teaser or appetizer to something much larger and grander, like an idea or product, that is trying to hook the target audience to go further. The word "whet" means to sharpen or make more keen, and in this context, describes how something can sharpen or increase one's desire for something. This phrase is usually used in relation to food to describe something that has made someone more hungry or eager to eat. However, it can also be used more broadly to describe anything that has increased someone's interest or desire. The origin of this idiom is not clear, but it's been used since the early 19th century.

## 22. Straw man

The term "straw man" refers to a rhetorical device where an argument or opponent's position is misrepresented or distorted in order to make it appear weaker or more easily refutable than it actually is. This is often used in debates, political discussions, and other forms of discourse as a way of discrediting an opposing viewpoint. The origins of the term "straw man" are traced back to the early 19th century when it was used in legal contexts. When a person was unable to pay a debt, a straw man would be used as a front for the debtor, with the straw man taking on the debt in their name. This would allow the debtor to avoid paying the debt and the creditor to avoid losing the money. The phrase "man of straw" is also related to the straw man concept, and it's used to describe a person who is weak, insubstantial, or easily swayed. The phrase is thought to have originated from the practice of using a straw man as a front for a debtor, as a straw man is seen as weak and insubstantial.

## 23. Deer in the headlights

The saying "deer in the headlights" refers to someone who is surprised or stunned by something and is unable to react or respond. The bright lights of a car can cause a deer to freeze in place, unable to move or react, and this is similar to the way that a person might freeze or become unable to react when faced with something unexpected or frightening. The earliest written use of this phrase dates back to the mid-20th century. It appears in the book *The New Dictionary of American Slang* by Harold Wentworth and Stuart Berg Flexner, which was published in 1960.

## 24. Go over with a fine tooth comb

The phrase "go over with a fine-tooth comb" is an expression that means to examine something very carefully or thoroughly. The origins come from the practice of using a comb with fine teeth to comb through hair or fibers to remove tangles or debris. The term originated in the late 19th century and has been used to describe the act of scrutinizing something with great attention to detail. It is also used to describe the process of searching for something specific or identifying errors or problems in a detailed manner.

## 25. Dark horse

The term "dark horse" is an expression that refers to a person (or a group, idea, technology, etc.) that is unexpected or unknown, but has the potential to become successful. The origin of the phrase comes from horse racing, specifically, a horse that is not well-known or has not previously competed, but has the potential to win the race. The phrase originated in the early 19th century, with the earliest known reference to the phrase in Benjamin Disraeli's novel *The Young Duke* in 1831, where he wrote: "A dark horse, which had never been thought of... rushed past the grandstand in sweeping triumph."

## 26. Cheapskate

The word "cheapskate" is a derogatory term used to describe someone who is excessively frugal or miserly. It suggests that the person is unwilling to spend money or is always looking for ways to save or cut costs, even when it is not necessary. There are a few theories about the origin of the word "cheapskate." One possibility is that it originated from the combination of the words "cheap" and "skate," which were both used to describe someone who was dishonest or unreliable. In this context, a "cheapskate" might be someone who was dishonest or unwilling to pay their fair share. Another theory is that it evolved from the phrase "cheap skate," which referred to a type of shoe that was made of cheap materials and was prone to falling apart. In this context, someone who was a "cheapskate" might be someone who was always trying to save money by buying cheap, low-quality goods.

# 27. Hit the books

The idiom "hit the books" means to intensely study or work hard on a project. It is often used to describe a situation where someone is making a concerted effort to learn something or to prepare for an exam or test. The origins of this idiom are not clear, but it has been in use since the mid-20th century. It is likely that the phrase is related to similar phrases that use "hit" as a way of expressing the start of something, such as "hit the trail" or "hit the road." When someone "hits the books," they are usually studying, reading, or preparing for something with a long bout of determination and focus.

## 28. In the doghouse

In 1911's *Peter Pan*, written by J.M. Barrie, Mr. Darling punishes himself for allowing his children to be kidnapped by sleeping in the dog's kennel. While this would be a great origin story for the idiom, it's not feasible, as the word 'doghouse' was not used in Scotland, where Barrie was born, or in England, where he lived. The idiom first appeared in writing in 1926 in J.J. Finerty's *Criminalese*, a dictionary of criminal language. The phrase had been used prior but in a much more literal meaning. It became a famous saying in the United States in the 1930s. Today, the phrase is used more figuratively to describe someone who is in trouble or has been scolded or reprimanded. For instance, a spouse might be "in the doghouse" for failing to do any household duties or an employee might be reprimanded and "in the doghouse" at their job, meaning their boss is viewing them unfavorably.

## 29. Lots of moving parts

The idiom "lots of moving parts" is a phrase that describes the complexity of a system, process, or task that has multiple interrelated components that are constantly changing or interacting with each other. The origins of this idiom are rooted in the manufacturing or mechanical industry, where the concept of a machine with many moving parts that must work together seamlessly in order for the machine to function effectively, is a common one.

## 30. Cry wolf

The term "to cry wolf" is used to describe a situation where someone raises a false alarm or makes a false claim in order to gain attention or deceive others. The phrase originated from Aesop's ancient Greek fable "The Boy Who Cried Wolf" in which a boy repeatedly cries "wolf!" when there is no wolf, causing the villagers to ignore him when a real wolf comes. The phrase is also used to indicate that someone's credibility is in question because of their history of raising false alarms or making false claims. This phrase is a cautionary tale, it serves as a reminder to be honest and truthful in our communication and not to abuse people's trust.

# Did You Know?

Shakespeare was born in Stratford-upon-Avon in 1564 to John Shakespeare, a successful glove-maker, and Mary Arden, the daughter of a well-to-do farmer. He was the third of eight children, and little is known about his childhood and education. However, it is believed that he received a good education and was well-versed in classical literature and the Bible.

In 1582, Shakespeare married Anne Hathaway, and they had three children together. In 1590, he moved to London to pursue a career in the theater, where he began working as an actor and writer. He quickly established himself as one of the most talented playwrights of his time, and his plays were performed at the Globe Theatre and the Blackfriars Theatre.

Throughout his career, Shakespeare wrote a wide variety of plays, including comedies, tragedies, and historical dramas. Some of his most famous works include *Macbeth*, *Hamlet*, *Romeo and Juliet*, *Othello*, and *The Tempest*. His plays are known for their memorable characters, complex plots, rich language and themes of love, jealousy, power, revenge, and the human condition.

In addition to his plays, Shakespeare also wrote a collection of sonnets, which are widely regarded as some of the greatest poems in the English language. The sonnets explore themes of love, beauty, and the passage of time and they remain popular and widely studied to this day.

Shakespeare's influence on the English language and literature is immense, and his plays and poems continue to be widely read, performed, and studied. He is often referred to as the "Bard of Avon" and is considered one of the greatest writers in the English language. He died in 1616 and was buried in Stratford-upon-Avon, England. Nevertheless, his legacy lives on, and his works continue to captivate audiences and inspire new generations of writers and artists.

## 31. Monday morning quarterback

The term "Monday morning quarterback" is a disapproving expression that refers to an individual who engages in the practice of criticizing the decisions and actions of others, particularly in relation to an event that has already occurred. This person offers their analysis and critiques from the perspective of 20/20 hindsight, without having been subject to the pressure or constraints of the situation. The phrase comes from American football, as most games are played on Sunday, and it is easy to critique a quarterback's decisions in the heat of the moment from the vantage point of the following day. The term was first coined by Barry Wood, the Harvard football team quarterback, during a speech in 1931.

# 32. Off the cuff

The phrase "off the cuff" is commonly used to describe a type of speaking or performance that is done without prior preparation. The idiom is thought to have originated in the world of jazz music, where musicians would often improvise solos on the spot, playing "off the cuff" rather than from a written score. The saying was popularized in the 1920s and 1930s when jazz music was at its peak in America. Nowadays, unrehearsed remarks or an impromptu moment caught on camera is said to be an "off the cuff" moment.

## 33. Wrap your head around something

The phrase "wrap your head around something" means coming to terms with something that is complex or challenging to understand. It is frequently used to describe the effort of making sense of an idea or concept that is difficult to grasp. This idiom made its first appearance in the *British boys'* magazine in the 1920s and has since gained widespread usage throughout the United States. It is synonymous with the phrase "getting one's head around," which was in common use prior to the emergence of "wrapping one's head around" as a popular idiom.

## 34. Go down in flames

The expression "to go down in flames" originated in the early 20th century during World War I and World War II, when airplanes were first utilized in warfare. The phrase comes from the imagery of an airplane crashing and catching fire, creating a fiery and explosive scene. This metaphor was initially used to describe the failure of a military mission, particularly when an aircraft was shot down in combat and crashed. However, as the term gained popularity, it started to be used more broadly to describe any dramatic and complete failure or collapse, in fields such as business, politics, and personal life.

## 35. Stitch up

The idiom "stitch up" is a British expression that means to deceive or betray someone, or to arrange things in a way that is dishonest or unfair. It is often used in a negative or critical way to imply that someone has been treated unfairly. It came about in the early 20th century from one of two sources. The first theory is that it originated in the world of criminal or underworld activity, where it was used to describe the act of framing someone or setting them up for a crime they did not commit. In this context, the "stitching" would refer to the act of deceit or betrayal, and the term "stitch up" would be used to describe someone who has been the victim of a dishonest or underhanded plot. The second theory is that the phrase comes from the idea of mending or repairing something that has been torn or damaged. In this case, the "stitching" would refer to the act of mending or fixing something, and the phrase "stitch up" would be used to describe someone who was able to repair a situation or solve a problem in a clever or resourceful way.

# 36. Break a leg

The idiom "break a leg" is a well-known expression that is often used as a way of wishing someone good luck, especially before a performance or competition. The inceptions of "break a leg" trace back to theater performances, but the original phrasing might have come about one of two ways. In theater, it was traditionally considered bad luck to wish someone "good luck." As a result, actors and actresses would instead use the phrase "break a leg" as a way of wishing each other luck without actually saying the words "good luck." Another theory is that the phrase may have started as a way of wishing someone luck by hoping that they would be successful enough to "break a leg" on stage, as this would be seen as a sign of a successful performance. Despite the uncertain origins of the phrase, "break a leg" has become a widely used expression in many English-speaking countries, and it is often used as a way of wishing someone good luck in a variety of different situations.

## 37. Like a cakewalk

The saying "like a cakewalk" means that something is very easy or effortless. The term is often used to describe a task or situation that requires little effort. The phrase is thought to have originated in the United States in the late 19th century and is often used colloquially in a lighthearted or humorous way. The word "cakewalk" originally referred to a type of dance popular in the late 19th century, characterized by its smooth and elegant style. It is thought that the phrase "like a cakewalk" evolved from this, with the idea being that something that is easy or effortless is similar to the graceful and easy-going nature of the cakewalk dance.

## 38. Run around in circles

The idiom "run around in circles" refers to a situation in which someone is making a lot of effort, but is not making any progress. It originated in the 19th century and likely developed from the literal practice of running in circles as a way to warm up or exercise. Today, it's often used to describe a situation in which someone is wasting their time or energy without achieving any results. The phrase can be applied to a variety of situations, such as trying to solve a problem or achieve a goal.

## 39. Get bent out of shape

"To get bent out of shape" means to become agitated or upset. It is often used to describe someone who becomes overly anxious or worked up about a situation that is not necessarily a big deal. Some sources suggest that the earliest meaning of the phrase was related to intoxication with alcohol, with "bent" being used to describe someone who was "drunk." As the decades progressed, the word "bent" was more commonly used to refer to someone getting upset. By the mid-1950s, the idiom was being used in its current form to describe someone who becomes agitated or upset due to stress or pressure.

# 40. Hunky dory

When everything's "hunky dory," everything is just fine. This expression first appeared in the United States in the 1860s when a Union soldier wrote to his family to tell them he was safe. Although it's unclear exactly where it originated, the word "hunk" was slang for a "safe place." The "dory" could be attributed to wordplay to give the term a singsong tone. Another explanation for the term was that it was brought back by sailors who had traveled to Japan in the 1850s to engage in trade. Honcho Dori Street in Yokohama was a popular destination for sailors; its streets were lined with establishments where sailors could enjoy themselves. It's said that the sailors, not familiar with the Japanese language, nicknamed the road Hunky-Dory and associated it with a place where everything was just fine.

Did You Know?

Confucius was a Chinese philosopher and teacher who lived in the Eastern Zhou period (5th century BC) in ancient China. He is one of the most influential figures in Chinese history and his teachings and ideas have had a profound impact on Chinese culture, politics, and philosophy.

Confucius was born in 551 BC in Qufu, Shandong province in China. He was born into a poor family, but he was highly intelligent and showed a keen interest in learning from a young age. He studied a wide variety of subjects, including literature, music, history, and the arts, and he later became a teacher, sharing his knowledge and wisdom with others.

Confucius believed in the importance of education and personal development. He believed that individuals could achieve moral and ethical excellence through self-discipline and the pursuit of knowledge. He also believed in the importance of family values, such as filial piety, and he encouraged people to cultivate good relationships with others through honesty, fairness, and respect.

Confucius' teachings were recorded by his disciples in a collection of texts known as the *Analects*. The *Analects* contain a wide range of Confucius' ideas, including his thoughts on education, ethics, and politics, and they remain an important source of Chinese philosophy to this day.

Confucius' impact on Chinese culture and history is immense, and his teachings continue to be widely studied and revered. He is the founder of

Confucianism, one of the major philosophical schools of ancient China, and his ideas have influenced a wide variety of fields, including politics, education, and ethics. Confucius' legacy lives on, and he remains one of the most important figures in Chinese history and culture.

## 41. Rat race

The term "rat race" originated from the practice of placing rats in circular cages and observing them as they run in a seemingly endless pursuit for a reward. In the real world, the phrase is used to describe the competitive and hectic nature of modern urban life, especially in the context of work and career. The expression implies that people are caught up in a meaningless, endless, and frantic pursuit of success and material wealth, akin to rats running in a maze in search of a reward. The rats would spend more energy than the reward is worth in the process, in a futile and mad competition.

## 42. Knock yourself out

The phrase "knock yourself out" is a colloquial expression that means "go ahead" or "do what you want," often used to give someone permission or encouragement. It can also be used to express sarcasm or irony, especially when trying to do something that is unnecessary. The term originated in the 20th century from the practice of boxers knocking themselves out in the ring. It can also be used in the sense of someone doing an activity to the point of exhaustion, as in knocking oneself out trying to do something.

## 43. Move heaven and earth

The idiom "move heaven and earth" conveys the idea of making a great effort or going to great lengths to accomplish something. The term probably came into use in the 1700s. Despite its uncertain origin, there are a few theories as to where it may have originated from. One theory is that the it's related to Archimedes' statement "Give me a lever long enough and a fulcrum on which to place it, and I shall move the world." However, it is worth noting that Archimedes lived in the 200s BC and the idiom did not come into use until two thousand years later. Another theory attributes the idiom to a passage in the Bible, Haggai 2:6: "… I will shake the heavens, and the earth, and the sea, and the dry land…" However, the word "move" is not an accurate synonym of the word "shake" in this context. Nowadays, when people say they will "move heaven and earth," it is often a statement that implies that the person won't give up and use whatever strength and resources they have to reach a goal.

## 44. Born with a silver spoon in their mouth

Someone "born with a silver spoon in their mouth" is a person who is born into a life of wealth and has had a privileged upbringing, never having to work for their wealth or status. The earliest printed record of the term is in Peter Anthony Motteux's translation of the novel *Don Quixote*, 1719: "Mum, Teresa, quoth Sancho, 'tis not all Gold that glisters, and every man was not born with a silver spoon in his mouth." The phrase implies that the person has had every advantage in life and has never had to work hard for their success. The phrase is thought to have originated in the 18th century, specifically from the custom of wealthy godparents gifting silver spoons to their godchildren as a symbol of wealth and good fortune. The British aristocracy used silverware when dining, which is why the phrase is speculated to have originated from the spoons.

## 45. Nip in the bud

The idiom "nip in the bud" describes the act of preventing something from developing or becoming a bigger problem by dealing with it at an early stage. The phrase is often used in the context of stopping a conflict or issue before it has a chance to grow or become more serious. The origin of the expression is derived from gardening, where it is common practice to cut off the buds of a plant before they have a chance to develop into flowers or fruits, in order to prevent the plant from wasting energy on unnecessary growth.

# 46. A stone's throw

The idiom "a stone's throw" is used to indicate that something is situated very close to another location. The phrase suggests that the distance between two places is so short that a stone could be thrown from one place to the other. The origins of this expression can be traced back to ancient times, when stones were commonly used as a weapon, and were thrown by hand or with a sling. Early English versions of the Bible also refer to "a stone's cast" with the same meaning, as in Luke 22:41, Wycliffe's Bible, 1526: "he gat himself from them, about a stone's cast."

## 47. Close shave

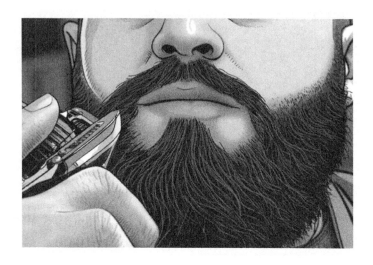

The phrase "close shave" means to narrowly avoid danger or a difficult situation. The origins of the phrase can be traced back to the act of shaving, specifically the use of a straight razor, which required skill and precision to avoid cutting oneself. The words "a close shave" were first recorded in 1825 and are considered an Americanism. In modern times, you could use the term "a close call" and "a close shave" interchangeably.

## 48. Tongue-in-cheek

The idiom "tongue-in-cheek" is used like an adjective to describe a statement or remark that is not meant to be taken seriously, often being made in a humorous or playful way. One theory of its origin is that it comes from sailing culture, referring to the practice of sailors putting their tongue in the cheek to indicate to their fellow sailors that they are joking or not to take their statement seriously. The first recorded use of the phrase in literature is from Scottish novelist Sir Walter Scott's 1828 book *The Fair Maid of Perth*, where the gesture of tongue-in-cheek is described, but it's not clear if it was intended to mean "not really." However, the use of the phrase in its modern sense is more clearly seen in a later citation by English poet Richard Barham in his 1845 collection of stories and poems *The Ingoldsby Legends* where the term is used to indicate sarcasm and irony. In this day and age, people might post "tongue-in-cheek" comments online or friends could make "tongue-in-cheek" remarks to each other while everyone knows what is being said isn't to be take seriously.

## 49. Spitting image

The term "spitting image" is used to describe someone who closely resembles another person, usually a parent or ancestor. The phrase became popular in the late 19th century, but the concept and expression was in circulation as early as 1689, when George Farquhar used it in his play *Love and a Bottle*: "Poor child! He's as like his own dada as if he were spit out of his mouth."

## 50. Hump day

The term "hump day" refers to the middle of the workweek, specifically Wednesday for most folks, which is often considered the "hump" to get over in order to reach the end of the week and the weekend. The phrase is often used in a lighthearted and humorous manner to help motivate people to push through the middle of the week. The term was popular in the 1980s but gained even more traction in 2013, when GEICO (an insurance company) created a popular commercial featuring a camel named "Cameron the Camel" strolling around an office and asking coworkers what day it was. The commercial ended with the punchline, "It's hump day!" After the commercial aired, the phrase became widely used and popularized as a way to refer to Wednesday.

# Did You Know?

Socrates was a classical Greek philosopher and is considered the founder of Western philosophy. He lived in Athens, Greece from 470-399 BC and is best known for his method of inquiry, known as the Socratic method, which involves asking questions to encourage critical thinking and problem solving. Socrates left no written works and much of what we know about him comes from the writings of his students, Plato and Xenophon.

Socrates was born in Athens to a family of modest means. He served as a hoplite (a type of infantryman) in the Athenian army during the Peloponnesian War, and it is said that he performed with bravery and distinction. After the war, Socrates turned to philosophy, and he spent the rest of his life engaging in philosophical dialogues and discussions with the people of Athens.

Socrates was a man of great integrity and courage. He was known for his unwavering commitment to the pursuit of wisdom and the importance of self-reflection. He believed that the only true wisdom was the knowledge of one's own ignorance and that it was only through questioning and examining one's own beliefs that true wisdom could be achieved. This approach to philosophy became known as the Socratic method, and it has had a profound impact on Western thought and culture.

One of the most famous episodes in the life of Socrates is his trial and execution. He was charged with corrupting the youth of Athens and impiety, and he was sentenced to death by drinking hemlock. Socrates was given the opportunity to escape, but he refused, stating that he would not betray his principles for the sake of his own life. His death is considered a turning point in Western thought and has become a symbol of the struggle for intellectual freedom and the pursuit of wisdom.

## 51. See eye to eye

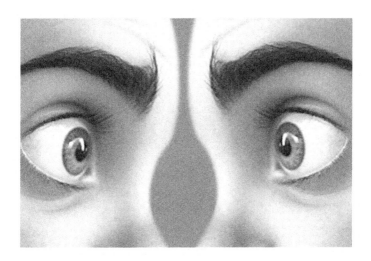

To "see eye to eye" is an idiom that indicates that two or more people are in agreement or understanding on a particular matter. The origins of this phrase date back to the 16th century, where it was used to describe a situation where people were able to look each other in the eyes as a way of expressing mutual understanding. The phrase, however, was taken from a biblical passage, Isaiah chapter 52 verse 8 of the King James Version: "...for they shall see eye to eye, when the Lord shall bring again Zion." In this passage, the expression see eye to eye means to meet face-to-face, or in person.

## 52. Beat around the bush

"Beat around the bush" is an idiom that means to avoid or evade a topic, often by talking about unrelated matters. It suggests that someone is being unnecessarily indirect or vague in their communication, and that they are avoiding or sidestepping an issue rather than addressing it directly. The phrase is thought to have originated in the 16th century. In modern usage, it's often used to describe situations where someone is being deceptive in their communication and avoiding the real issue at hand.

## 53. Bob's your uncle

The idiom "Bob's your uncle" is an odd British phrase indicating that something is easy or simple to do. It is often used to give instructions or to express that the completion of a task is guaranteed. The phrase originated in the late 19th century and is believed to have been first used by British Prime Minister Robert Cecil, also known as Lord Salisbury. According to popular legend, Lord Salisbury appointed his nephew, Arthur Balfour, to the position of Chief Secretary when he was the Prime Minister and said, "And there you are, Bob's your uncle!" to indicate that the appointment was a done deal.

## 54. The whole nine yards

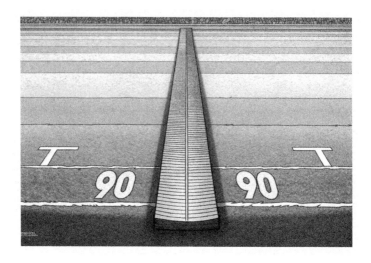

The exact origins of the idiom "the whole nine yards" are not clear and there are two main theories about where it comes from. The first theory refers to the amount of fabric needed to make a traditional Scottish kilt, which is nine yards, suggesting that the idiom originally referred to someone who was fully dressed in traditional Scottish attire, including the kilt. The second theory refers to the amount of ammunition that a fighter aircraft could carry, which was also nine yards, suggesting that the expression originally referred to someone who was fully armed and equipped for battle. Regardless of its origins, the idiom "the whole nine yards" has been used since the 1960s and means that something is done completely or thoroughly.

## 55. High and mighty

The expression "high and mighty" is often used to describe someone who acts arrogant and superior, exhibiting a sense of self-importance and a tendency to look down on others. This person may treat others with disdain or contempt as if they believe themselves to be "higher" and "mightier" in some way. The phrase has a long history, with one of the earliest recorded uses dating back to the letter written in 1420 by Robert Waterton to King Henry V. In the letter, King Henry is referred to as a "right excellent high and right mighty Prince and most dreaded sovereign Lord." This suggests that the phrase has been used for centuries to describe those who hold themselves in high regard and believe to be superior to others. In modern times, the idiom "high and mighty" is often used to describe individuals who exhibit arrogant or pretentious behavior, which is generally considered a negative trait.

## 56. A dime a dozen

The idiom "a dime a dozen" refers to something that is abundant and ubiquitous, thus considered inexpensive or of little value. The phrase originates from the fact that a dime is a unit of US currency that is worth ten cents. The dime coin was first minted in 1796, and in the 1800s, many goods, such as eggs or apples, were advertised as costing a dime a dozen in the United States, indicating they were being sold at good value for the money. However, over time, the meaning of the phrase evolved to indicate the opposite, referring to something that is nearly worthless due to its commonness and easy availability. The first recorded use of the expression in this context was in 1930 and continues to be used in the same way today.

## 57. Yellow

The idiom "yellow" means to be cowardly or lacking in courage. It originated in the early 20th century and comes from the idea of the color yellow being associated with cowardice or treachery. There are a few different theories about how the color yellow came to be associated with cowardice. One theory is that it originated in the military, where soldiers who were considered to be brave or courageous would wear red or blue uniforms, while those who were considered to be less brave or cowardly would wear yellow. Another theory is that the association may have come from the way that some animals, such as chickens, are known to turn yellow when they are frightened or stressed. Regardless of its origins, the word "yellow" is now widely used in English in a derogatory or mocking way to imply that someone is afraid or lacks the courage to do something.

## 58. Sell like hot cakes

The idiom "sell like hot cakes" is used to describe a situation where something is in high demand and is selling quickly. It likely originated from the popularity of hot cakes as a breakfast food in the United States in the 19th and early 20th centuries. In this context, the phrase "sell like hot cakes" referred to the ease with which hot cakes were sold due to their popularity. The phrase is now used more broadly to refer to any situation where a product or service is highly sought-after and selling at a fast pace. It can be used to describe a variety of items, such as products, services, and tickets for events.

## 59. The jig is up

The phrase "the jig is up" is used to express that a deception or a secret has been discovered, and that the person responsible is likely to be caught or held accountable. The phrase originated in the late 19th century, however the exact etymology is uncertain. One theory suggests that it comes from the word "jig" which was a slang term for a deception or a trick, and that when the "jig is up," the trick has been discovered. Another theory is that it comes from the dance, "jig," where the music would stop and the dancers would be caught if they were doing something wrong.

# 60. Shed light on

The idiomatic expression "to shed light on" means to provide information or understanding about something, to make something clear, or to reveal something that was previously unknown or difficult to understand. The origins of the phrase can be traced back to the everyday act of lighting a room or space with a candle or fire. The act of illuminating a space was known as "shedding light" in Europe, thus the term came to be used to describe the clearing of doubts or the making of a complicated situation clearer.

# Did You Know?

Aesop was a legendary ancient Greek storyteller who lived between 620-560 BC. Although not much is known about his life, his tales have been popular and widely read for centuries. Aesop's fables are a collection of stories, each with a moral lesson, and are meant to educate and entertain the audience. The tales feature animals with human-like characteristics and often reflect on universal truths and wisdom.

The exact origins of Aesop's fables are not known and the storyteller himself is shrouded in mystery. Some historical accounts suggest that he was born a slave in Thrace and later freed by his master, while others claim that he was born free in Phrygia. Regardless of his origins, Aesop became famous for his wit, wisdom, and storytelling skills, as he traveled throughout Greece to tell his tales.

Aesop's fables have been passed down from generation to generation and have been translated into many languages. The tales are known for their simple, yet profound, messages and have been used as a means of teaching moral values to children and adults alike. Some of the most famous fables include "The Ant and the Grasshopper," "The Tortoise and the Hare," and "The Boy Who Cried Wolf."

## 61. Gloves are off

The idiom "the gloves are off" connotes the removal of constraints or inhibitions and the readiness to engage in a fight (either physically or figuratively). The origins of this phrase are likely rooted in the practice of removing gloves before engaging in a physical fight. It is commonly associated with boxing gloves and the increased brutality and damage that would occur in a match without them. However, an earlier variant of the idiom, "to handle someone without gloves," was in use since the early 1800s and shared a similar meaning of dealing with someone in a rough and uncompromising way. Since boxing with gloves was uncommon until the late 1800s, it appears that the idiom does not specifically derive from boxing but rather from the allusion to men taking their gloves off to prepare for a serious and possibly violent confrontation. In more polite society, a person might say "the gloves are coming off" before they tackle a big project at work or a tough task that requires a lot of effort.

## 62. Land of milk and honey

The "land of milk and honey" is a colloquial expression that means a place of abundance and prosperity, often used to describe a utopia or paradise. The phrase is often used in a metaphorical sense to describe a place where everything is perfect and everything is available in abundance. It originates from the Hebrew Bible, specifically in the book of Exodus, where God promised the Israelites that he would lead them to a land flowing with milk and honey: "And I am come down to deliver them out of the hand of the Egyptians, and to bring them up out of that land unto a good land and a large, unto a land flowing with milk and honey…" The expression is also found in the book of Numbers and Leviticus.

## 63. Bone to pick

The idiom "bone to pick" means to have a disagreement or issue to resolve. The phrase is often used as "to have a bone to pick with (someone)," which means to have a specific issue or problem that needs to be addressed with that person. Most sources state that this expression comes from a dog trying to pick off the meat from a bone, and one connotation of this idiom is trying to solve a difficult, time-consuming problem. This is likely related to the fact that dogs often gnaw on a bone for very long periods of time, even when most of the meat is gone. This type of usage dates back to the 1500s. The other more common connotation of the phrase is to try to settle a dispute with someone. This usage goes back to the 1800s. Alternatively, it might come from the idea of two dogs fighting over a bone.

## 64. By the skin of your teeth

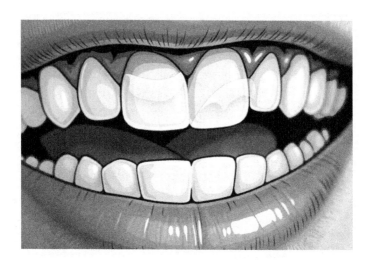

The idiom "by the skin of your teeth" refers to a situation in which someone barely succeeds or avoids something, often by a very narrow margin or with great difficulty. It originated in the 16th century and is likely derived from the Biblical phrase "delivered by the skin of their teeth," which appears in *The Book of Job*. Today, the term is used to convey a sense of narrow escape or close call.

# 65. Gray area

The term "gray area" refers to a situation or issue that is not clearly defined or that falls between two clearly defined categories or extremes. It is often used to describe something that is ambiguous or open to interpretation, or that is not easily classified as right or wrong. The origin of the phrase "gray area" is not entirely clear, but it is thought to have originated in the 20th century. One theory is that it originated from the use of the color gray to represent neutrality or ambiguity. Another theory is that the phrase originated in the field of psychology, where it was used to describe a range of behaviors or experiences that fall between normal and abnormal. In this context, the "gray area" would refer to the range of behaviors or experiences that are not clearly defined as normal or abnormal, but that fall somewhere in between.

## 66. You can't have your cake and eat it too

The idiom "you can't have your cake and eat it too" is a well-known English expression that conveys the idea that one cannot have or enjoy all the benefits of a situation without having to accept the drawbacks or consequences as well. It is often used to indicate that one must make a choice between two mutually exclusive options. The origins of this idiom can be traced back to the early 1600s, with the earliest known written record of the phrase appearing in a poem by John Heywood in 1546. The same sentiment of the necessity of making a choice may be found in other idioms from different cultures, such as the Albanian proverb that says "you cannot take a swim and not get wet" or the German saying that states "you cannot dance at two weddings at the same time," "you can't make an omelette without breaking eggs" in French, and "you can't have the fruit and the seed" in Spanish.

In British English, the last word is often omitted from the proverb, as in "you can't have your cake and eat it."

## 67. Leave no stone unturned

The idiom "leave no stone unturned" means to make a thorough and exhaustive effort to achieve a goal or solve a problem. It suggests that the person or group in question is determined, persistent, and willing to explore every possible option or avenue to achieve their desired outcome. The story of its origin dates back to a Greek legend. A general of Xerxes named Mardonius was believed to have buried treasure near his tent. In 447 BC, when Mardonius was defeated at the battle of Plataea, Polycrates of Thebes began searching for the treasure to no avail. He consulted the Oracle of Delphi, who advised him to look under every stone. When the medieval scholar Erasmus translated the story into Latin, he quoted the Oracle as saying, "leave no stone unturned." Erasmus' work was translated into English in the 1500s, and the expression has been used since then.

## 68. Cooking the books

"Cooking the books" is an expression that refers to the act of falsifying or manipulating financial records or accounts in order to deceive or mislead others. It usually refers to accounting fraud, where companies falsify their financial statements to make them appear more profitable or financially stable than they really are. This can be done in various ways, such as by understating expenses, overstating revenues, or creating false entries in the financial records. This type of fraud can be committed by individuals within a company, and it can have serious consequences for investors, employees, and the company as a whole. The phrase has been used since the 17th century, as evidenced by the Earl of Strafford in his *Letters and Dispatches* from 1636, where he wrote, "The proof was once clear, however they have cook'd it since."

## 69. Jam on the brakes

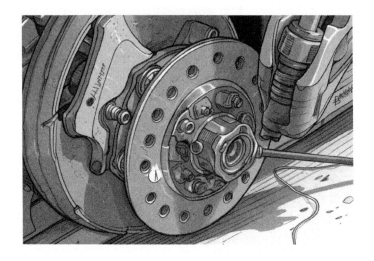

To "jam on the brakes" means to make a sudden, forceful stop, usually while driving a vehicle. It is often used to describe a sudden, unexpected stop or a stop made in an emergency situation. The origin of this idiom is thought to be related to the physical act of pressing down on the brake pedal of a vehicle in order to bring it to a stop. The metaphor suggests that one is making a sudden and forceful stop, much like one might press down hard on the brake pedal to bring a vehicle to a rapid stop. The earliest written use of this phrase dates back to the early 20th century. It appears in a book called *The Motor Boys on the Pacific* by Clarence Young, which was published in 1906. The book includes the line, "I just jammed on the brakes and stopped." In casual conversation, however, you could say to someone "let's jam on the breaks," meaning that they are talking too much and you want them to stop or they are going on and on about something that is making you uncomfortable and you need a break.

## 70. Needle in a haystack

The famous idiom "needle in a haystack" is a powerful metaphor that is used to describe an elusive or difficult-to-find object, situation, or information. It often conveys the idea that something is so insignificant or small in comparison to the larger surrounding area that it becomes almost impossible to locate. The origins of this phrase can be traced back to the practice of farming, where needles, which were handcrafted and made of materials that blended in with hay, were difficult to locate within a haystack. Another idiom with the word needle is "move the needle" which is a metaphor that describes a significant improvement or change in a situation or performance.

# Did You Know?

1. The word "quarantine" comes from the Italian "quaranta giorni," which means "forty days." The term originally described the practice of isolating ships that arrived in port for forty days to prevent the spread of infectious diseases.

2. The word "algebra" comes from the Arabic "al-jabr," which means "the reunion of broken parts." It was used by the mathematician Muhammad ibn Musa al-Khwarizmi to describe a system for solving equations.

3. The word "sarcasm" comes from the Greek "sarkasmos," which means "to tear flesh, bite the lip in rage, sneer." It originally referred to a sharp, bitter, or cutting remark.

4. The word "quark" comes from the German "quark," which means "curd." It was coined by the physicist Murray Gell-Mann to describe a type of subatomic particle.

# 71. To see red

The expression "to see red" is used to describe a feeling of extreme anger or rage. It originated in the early 20th century and is derived from the association of the color red with anger and violence. When someone is "seeing red," they are experiencing a strong emotional response characterized by intense anger and a desire to lash out. The phrase is often used to describe someone who is visibly upset and angry, and may be accompanied by physical signs of rage such as clenched fists, reddened face, and raised voice. It is typically used in a metaphorical sense and does not mean that someone is literally seeing the color red.

## 72. Tip of the iceberg

The "tip of the iceberg" refers to a small part of a larger problem or situation that is visible or apparent, but the vast majority remains hidden. It is used to convey the idea that what is visible is only a small part of a much larger issue. The idiom is often used in a negative context, to describe a situation where the true extent of a problem or issue is not immediately obvious. The origin of the phrase comes from the literal appearance of icebergs, which are large chunks of ice floating in the ocean. Only the top of the iceberg is visible above the waterline, while the vast majority of the iceberg remains hidden underwater. The first recorded use of the phrase in print is from a 1912 article in the *New York Times*, describing the sinking of the ocean liner RMS Titanic, which struck an iceberg and sank.

## 73. Draw a line in the sand

The idiomatic expression "draw a line in the sand" is a colloquial way of establishing a clear and decisive boundary or a point of no return. The origins of this phrase can be traced back to a number of historical references, such as in the Bible, where it refers to Jesus' writing in the sand, in the Ramayana where a circle was drawn around someone for protection, and in Roman history where the phrase was used to indicate a clear stance on a political issue. One of the most notable historical references is from 168 BC, when a Roman Consul named Gaius Popillius Laenas drew a circular line in the sand around King Antiochus IV of the Seleucid Empire, then said, "Before you cross this circle I want you to give me a reply for the Roman Senate" – implying that Rome would declare war if the King stepped out of the circle without committing to leave Egypt immediately. Weighing his options, Antiochus wisely decided to withdraw. Only then did Popillius agree to shake hands with him. In modern times, a person might "draw a line in the sand" in a relationship to unambiguously let the other person know what behaviors or actions they will not tolerate.

# 74. The final straw

The "the final straw" is derived from the phrase "the last straw that broke the camel's back." It refers to a situation where one last event or action causes a person to reach their breaking point and respond with a strong reaction, usually anger or frustration. It is often used in a situation where someone has tolerated a negative behavior for a long time, but one final event pushes them over the edge. The term "the last feather breaks the horse's back" is an earlier version of this idiom, dating back to the 1800s. The origin of the phrase comes from the old practice of loading heavy loads on the back of a camel or a donkey. The earliest example of the idiom can be found in *The Edinburgh Advertiser*, from May 1816, where the phrase is used in the context of a rich man who used camels to transport his straw. He would load as much straw as he could on them in order to get the most out of the animals. One day he proceeded to load one last piece of straw onto the camel's back and the camel collapsed.

## 75. Doesn't cut the mustard

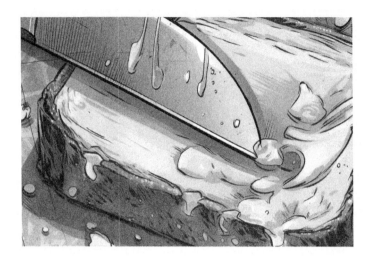

The odd idiom "doesn't cut the mustard" is used to convey that something or someone is not of sufficient quality or fails to meet the required standard. It implies that the person or thing being referred to is inadequate or unsatisfactory. The phrase is believed to have originated from the farming practice of cutting mustard, which was one of the main crops in East Anglia in Britain. Mustard was traditionally cut by hand with scythes, similar to corn. As the crop could grow up to six feet high, it required extremely sharp tools. When the tools were not sharp enough, they "would not cut the mustard" resulting in the work being more difficult and less efficient.

## 76. From the bottom of one's heart

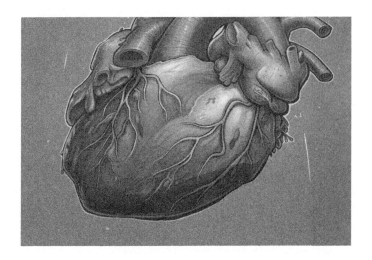

"From the bottom of one's heart" is an idiomatic expression that indicates that something is said or done with genuine sincerity and emotion. One theory about its origins is that it dates back to ancient Greece when the philosopher Archimedes mistakenly believed that the heart was responsible for thinking and feeling, while the brain pumped blood. According to this theory, this belief may have led to the idea that when something is said or done "from the bottom of one's heart," it is coming from a place of deep, genuine feeling.

## 77. Off the table

The idiom "off the table" is used to indicate that something is no longer being considered or is not an option anymore. It is often used in a negotiation or decision-making context to indicate that a particular proposal, idea, or option has been rejected or is no longer open for discussion. The phrase suggests that the item in question has been physically removed from the table, signifying that it is no longer under consideration. The origins of this idiom come from a literal meaning of taking something off a table so that the parties making a deal can't bicker over it further.

## 78. Round the bend

The expression "round the bend" means to be crazy or mentally unbalanced. It is often used to describe someone who is behaving in an irrational or unpredictable way, or who is showing signs of mental instability. The origin of this idiom is not clear, but it is thought to be related to the idea of going around a bend or curve in a road. The metaphor suggests that one is going off in an unexpected or unusual direction, much like a road might curve or bend unexpectedly. An early written use of this phrase dates back to the early 20th century. It appears in a book called *The Delectable Duchy* by Arthur Thomas Quiller-Couch, which was published in 1913. The book includes the line, "He had a good heart, and a clear head; but he was round the bend a little, as the saying is."

## 79. Make a mountain out of a molehill

The phrase "to make a mountain out of a molehill" is used to describe someone who is exaggerating the importance or seriousness of a situation, often making it seem much worse than it actually is. This expression originated in the 16th century, and is a metaphor that compares a small, insignificant problem to a large and imposing mountain. The oldest record of this idiom can be found in a book by Nicholas Udall in 1548, where he wrote. "The Sophists of Greece could through their copiousness make an Elephant of a fly and a mountain of a molehill," clearly illustrating the concept of exaggeration and the impossibility of comparing an elephant to a fly due to their vastly different sizes. Since then, this idiom has been widely used to highlight dramatization, where one side might say to the opposition that they are "making a mountain out of a molehill" out of a small issue.

# 80. Barrel of laughs

The expression "a barrel of laughs" means that something or someone is very amusing or entertaining. It is often said in a lighthearted or playful manner, indicating that the speaker finds the person or thing to be a source of joy or enjoyment. It is thought to have originated in the United States in the early 20th century and has been in widespread use since then. The phrase likely comes from the concept of a "barrel of monkeys," a toy consisting of small, plastic monkeys that are strung together and can be manipulated to form different shapes or configurations. The toy is known for being entertaining, particularly for children. It is likely that the phrase "a barrel of laughs" was originally used to describe something that was similarly amusing.

# Did You Know?

January is the first month of the year in our modern calendar. It is derived from the Latin "Januarius," which is named after the Roman god Janus, who was the god of beginnings and endings.

February is derived from the Latin "Februarius," which is named after the festival of Februa, a purification ritual that was held during the month.

March is derived from the Latin "Martius," which is named after the Roman god Mars, who was the god of war.

April is derived from the Latin "Aprilis," which is probably derived from the Greek word "apros," meaning "to open," as this was the time of year when plants and flowers began to open and bloom.

May is derived from the Latin "Maius," which is named after the Roman goddess Maia, who was the mother of Mercury, the messenger of the gods.

June is derived from the Latin "Junius," which is named after the Roman goddess Juno, who was the wife of Jupiter, the king of the gods.

## 81. Read between the lines

To "read between the lines" means to infer or interpret something that is not explicitly stated, often by looking for hidden meanings or subtext in a text or conversation. It is often used to suggest that there is more to something than meets the eye, or that one should consider multiple interpretations or perspectives. The origin of this idiom might be related to the idea of looking beyond the surface of something to discover its deeper meaning. The metaphor suggests that there are hidden meanings or messages "between the lines" of a text or conversation. The earliest written use of this phrase dates back to the mid-19th century. It appears in a letter written by the British poet Elizabeth Barrett Browning, which was published in a book called *The Letters of Elizabeth Barrett Browning* in 1906. In the letter, Barrett Browning writes, "I cannot help reading between the lines of your letter, and feeling that you are not perfectly well."

## 82. Preaching to the choir

The idiom "preaching to the choir" is a variation of the earlier phrase "preaching to the converted." The concept of preaching to those already in agreement with a particular belief or viewpoint can be traced back to an 1857 article in *The Times* which stated, "It is an old saying that to preach to the converted is a useless office, and I may add that to preach to the unconvertible is a thankless office." The modern iteration of the phrase, "preaching to the choir," is of American origin. The first recorded use of the phrase in this format can be found in 1973, in *The Lima News* in Ohio, where it was used to describe a minister preaching to regular church attendees rather than those in need of the message.

## 83. More bang for one's buck

The origin of the idiom "more bang for one's buck" can be traced back to the early 20th century, when "bang" was used as slang to refer to excitement or thrill. It is believed that the phrase was first used in the context of entertainment, such as carnivals or circuses, where one would want to get the most excitement or thrills for their money. The phrase then gained popularity during World War II, as the US military sought to make the most out of their limited resources. The military needed to maximize the effectiveness of their weapons and equipment and thus the phrase "more bang for one's buck" was used to refer to getting the most firepower for the amount of money or resources invested. The phrase then was adopted by civilians and has been used in various contexts such as business, marketing and everyday life. It is used to describe a product, service, or investment that offers a lot of features or benefits for a relatively low cost.

## 84. A win-win situation

The phrase "a win-win situation" refers to a scenario in which all parties benefit or are satisfied with the outcome. The metaphor suggests that all parties involved are able to "win," or achieve their goals. This isn't often the case in politics or business, but when both sides come out happy and satisfied that they got what they wanted it is a "win-win." The earliest written use of this phrase dates back to the late 20th century and it appears in a book called *The Psychology of Persuasion* by Robert B. Cialdini, which was published in 1984. The book includes the line, "In a win-win situation, everyone involved benefits."

## 85. On sixes and sevens

The idiom "on sixes and sevens" is used to describe a state of confusion or disorder. It can refer to a scene of overall chaos, or to describe a group of people who are unable to agree or make a decision. There are a few theories about the origin of this idiom. The first theory is that it originated in the 1300s. At that time, the phrase was "on six and seven," and it referred to a dice game in which a roll of six or seven meant that a player was risking their entire fortune. The second theory suggests that it may have originated in medieval England, where it was used to describe a state of disarray or confusion. The third theory is that it originated in ancient Rome, where the number six was considered unlucky and the number seven was lucky. The earliest written use of the phrase "on sixes and sevens" appears in a book called *The Proverbs, Epigrams, and Miscellanies* by John Heywood, which was published in 1562. The book includes the line, "As a man on six and seven, that knoweth not whether he be on horseback or on foot."

## 86. Fool's gold

The term "fool's gold" describes something that appears valuable, but is actually worthless. The phrase originated in the 19th century from the mining industry, where iron pyrite, a mineral that closely resembles gold, was often mistaken for the real thing by inexperienced prospectors. The name "fool's gold" was given to this mineral due to the fact that it often led to disappointment for those who mistook it for the real thing. Nowadays, an ill-advised investment, a sill technologic pursuit, or a misleading piece of advice could all be "fool's gold."

## 87. Batten down the hatches

The idiom "batten down the hatches" has its roots in the nautical world of medieval times, when ship travel was a common mode of transportation to new territories. The English used navies and ships to establish colonies around the world. The term literally refers to the practice of covering the openings on the deck of a ship, known as hatches, with tarpaulin and wooden strips called battens, in order to prevent water from entering the ship during bad weather. The sailors would refer to this activity as "battening down." The phrase has been in use since at least 1769, with references to it in *An Universal Dictionary of the Marine* by William Falconer. Despite variations in spelling of the word "batten" such as "battern" and "baton," the meaning of the phrase has remained the same. In modern times, you could "batten down the hatches" by boarding up or protecting your home or property before a storm, or the phrase can be used in a more figurative sense to prepare oneself for a coming struggle or confrontation.

## 88. Foul play

"Foul play" refers to dishonest or malicious actions, typically in the context of sports or games. It is thought to have originated in the sport of cricket, where it was used to describe actions that violated the rules of the game. In modern usage, the term is used more broadly to describe any situation where someone has acted dishonestly in order to gain an advantage. It's colloquially used in reference to criminal investigations, where it may be suggested that a crime was committed in a premeditated manner. The phrase is often used as a warning or cautionary message, indicating that someone or something may be acting in a way that is not above board or that may be harmful to others.

## 89. Something has legs

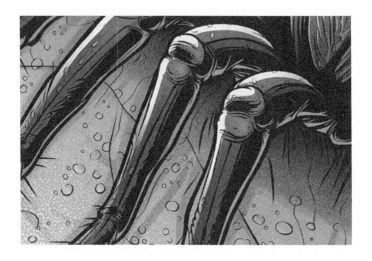

To say that "something has legs" indicates that an idea or a situation has the potential to grow or develop. The phrase originated in the early 20th century, and is based on the imagery of something that can carry itself forward on its legs. It's often used to describe an idea or a situation that has the potential to be successful or have a long-term impact.

## 90. Bend over backwards

If you "bend over backwards" you are making a very strong or extreme effort to do something, often in order to help or accommodate someone else. This idiom originated in the United States in the 20th century and comes from the literal act of bending over backwards, which is a very difficult and strenuous physical position to maintain. The phrase suggests that the person in question is making an immense effort to accomplish something, often to the point of straining themselves or going to great lengths to achieve their goal. Today, the idiom is frequently used in a positive or complimentary way, implying that a person is going above and beyond to assist others.

# Did You Know?

July is derived from the Latin "Julius," which is named after Julius Caesar, the Roman general and statesman.

August is derived from the Latin "Augustus," which is named after Augustus Caesar, the first Roman emperor.

September is derived from the Latin "September," which means "seventh" in Latin, as it was originally the seventh month of the Roman calendar.

October is derived from the Latin "October," which means "eighth" in Latin, as it was originally the eighth month of the Roman calendar.

November is derived from the Latin "November," which means "ninth" in Latin, as it was originally the ninth month of the Roman calendar.

December is derived from the Latin "December," which means "tenth" in Latin, as it was originally the tenth month of the Roman calendar.

## 91. Diamond in the rough

The phrase "diamond in the rough" refers to someone or something that has potential or value, but is not yet fully developed or polished. The origin of the phrase comes from the process of diamond mining, where a diamond in its natural state, before it is cut and polished, is often referred to as a "rough diamond." This term was used as early as the 1600s and it first appeared in print in John Fletcher's 1624 play *A Wife for a Month*, where it is written, "She is very honest, and will be as hard to cut as a rough diamond." One fun fact about diamonds is that they are made up of pure carbon, the same element that makes up graphite in pencils. However, the unique way in which the carbon atoms are arranged in a diamond gives it its exceptional strength and durability, as well as its iconic sparkle and brilliance. Nowadays, we might say that a person with budding talent but is yet unknown or a product that hasn't taken off yet are "diamonds in the rough."

## 92. In for a penny in for a pound

The idiom "in for a penny, in for a pound" refers to a situation in which someone decides to fully commit to a task or venture, even if it requires a significant amount of time, effort, or resources. It originated in the 17th century and is derived from the phrase "all in for a penny, all in for a pound," which was used to describe the act of gambling with a small amount of money in the hope of winning a larger amount. Today the expression is often used to convey a sense of determination or commitment.

## 93. Be in a tight corner

To "be in a tight corner" means to be in a difficult situation. It often describes a circumstance in which someone is facing challenges or problems that are hard to overcome. There are two different theories about the origins of this phrase. The first is that it comes from the idea of being trapped or cornered in a physical sense, such as being trapped in a small space or against a wall, suggesting that the idiom originally referred to the feeling of being physically trapped or confined. The second is related to the expression "in a bind," which means to be in a difficult or challenging situation, suggesting that the idiom originally referred to the idea of being caught or trapped in a difficult situation that is hard to escape from.

## 94. Build castles in the sky

To say that a person wants "to build castles in the sky" means that they have unrealistic or impractical plans or ideas. It suggests that the person is constructing something that is not based in reality and has no solid foundation. This phrase is often used to criticize someone for being overly optimistic or for having unrealistic expectations. This idiom originated in the 1500s and evolved from the original phrase "to build castles in Spain." During this time, much of Spain was under Moorish* control and the idea of building a castle there was considered to be an unattainable dream.

*During the Middle Ages, the term "Moor" was utilized by Christian Europeans to denote the Muslim inhabitants of the Maghreb, the Iberian Peninsula, Sicily, and Malta.

## 95. Blessing in disguise

The idiom "blessing in disguise" refers to something that seems bad or unfortunate at first, but ultimately turns out to have a positive outcome or result. The origin of this phrase can be traced back to the hymn, "Since all the downward tracts of time" by James Hervey, which was first published in 1746. In this hymn, Hervey meditated on the wisdom of accepting whatever God chose to bestow on us, even things that seemed negative or undesirable at first, because they might ultimately be "blessings in disguise," or good things that were initially difficult to recognize as such due to their appearance or circumstances. This expression has been in use since the mid-1700s and is a way of looking on the bright side of a challenging situation and finding the silver lining within.

## 96. Hunker down

The term "hunker down" has its origins in the American South in the 19th century, and is believed to be derived from the Scottish word "hunk," meaning to crouch or huddle. Initially used as a hunting term, describing the act of crouching low to the ground to avoid detection from prey, it gradually transitioned to a more general meaning of settling in for a long wait or preparing for a difficult situation. During World War II, soldiers were instructed to "hunker down" in trenches to avoid enemy fire, which further popularized the phrase. Today, it is commonly used to describe the act of preparing for a challenge or bracing oneself for a difficult situation, whether it be a natural disaster, a tough project, or a trying period in life.

## 97. In two shakes of a lamb's tail

The phrase "in two shakes of a lamb's tail" is a colloquial expression that originated in the early 19th century. The idiom is thought to be a variation of "in two shakes of a dead lion's tail" which was used to indicate something that would happen quickly or without delay. The phrase is used to indicate something that will happen quickly or immediately, similar to how fast a lamb's tail can be shaken twice. Interestingly, the term "shake" is an informal unit of time, which was first named and defined by the scientists working on the Manhattan Project*. These scientists designated a shake to be equal to ten nanoseconds, as they needed to be able to measure time in small increments in order to describe nuclear reactions. The earliest known publication of the expression "in two shakes of a lamb's tail" was in *Ingoldsby Legends* by Richard Barham in 1840. However, it is likely that the phrase is older than that, but its exact etymology is currently unknown.

*The Manhattan Project was a top-secret research and development program during World War II, which resulted in the creation of the world's first nuclear weapons. The project was headed by the United States and received support from the United Kingdom and Canada.

## 98. Over my dead body

If someone utters the phrase "over my dead body," it means that they strongly oppose or object to something. It is often used to express determination to prevent something from happening. The term may have originated in the 16th century, and it is said to have been used by knights when discussing the treasure that they had sworn to protect. In this context, the saying suggests that the enemy would have to walk over their dead body to reach the treasure. This is not the common usage of the expression, and it is not the way in which it is now used. Today, the idiom is often used in a more dramatic or exaggerated way to express strong opposition or determination, and it's not meant to be taken literally.

## 99. Couch potato

The term "couch potato" is used to describe a person who is lazy and inactive, often spending most of their time sitting on a couch watching television. It originated in the 1970s in America, coined by a comic artist who drew two idle and lazy characters which he named "Couch Potatoes." The phrase quickly caught on and is now commonly used to refer to those who lead a sedentary lifestyle. The term "couch potato" is a playful and humorous way of describing someone who is lazy and inactive, and is often used in a lighthearted or teasing manner.

# 100. Jump ship

If someone is ready to "jump ship" then they are about to abandon a situation, particularly a job or a project, without warning. The origin of this phrase comes from the practice of sailors deserting a ship, often by jumping off into the water and swimming to shore. This was a dangerous and potentially deadly action, as sailors could be left stranded in the middle of the ocean or face harsh punishment if caught. The expression became popular as a metaphor for leaving a situation in the early 20th century, and has been in common usage since then.

# Did You Know?

The longest words in the English language are:

1. Honorificabilitudinitatibus (twenty-seven letters) is a word that refers to the state of being able to achieve honor. It is not a commonly used word and is mostly found in lists of long words or in discussions about the history of the English language.

2. Antidisestablishmentarianism (twenty-eight letters) refers to opposition to the disestablishment of the Church of England, especially in the 19th century. This word is not often used in everyday conversation, but it may come up in discussions about the history of the Church of England or the separation of church and state.

3. Floccinaucinihilipilification (twenty-nine letters) is a word that refers to the act of estimating something as worthless. It is not a commonly used word and is mostly found in lists of long words.

4. Supercalifragilisticexpialidocious (thirty-four letters) is a word that is used to describe something extraordinary or wonderful. It is famously used in the song "Supercalifragilisticexpialidocious" from the movie *Mary Poppins*. The word is not used often in everyday conversation, but it is recognized by many people due to the popular song.

5. Pneumonoultramicroscopicsilicovolcanoconiosis (forty-five letters) is a technical term used to describe a lung disease caused by inhaling very fine silica particles. It is not a commonly used word and is often

listed as one of the longest words in the English language.

## 101. Have the blues

To "have the blues" means you have a feeling of sadness or melancholy. It originated in the United States in the early 20th century, specifically in African American communities in the southern states. The phrase is thought to be derived from the musical genre known as the blues, which emerged at around the same time and is characterized by its emotive, soulful lyrics and themes of heartbreak, loneliness, and the struggles of daily life. It is possible that the expression was originally used to describe someone who was feeling down or depressed, possibly because they were listening to or performing blues music. Over time, the phrase became more popular and came to be used more broadly to describe any feeling of sadness or depression. Today, the idiom is commonly used in casual conversation to refer to a general feeling of melancholy, regardless of its connection to the blues genre.

**Bonus!**

Thanks for supporting me and purchasing this book! I'd like to send you some freebies. They include:

- The digital version of *500 World War I & II Facts*

- The digital version of *101 Idioms and Phrases*

- The audiobook for my best seller *1144 Random Facts*

Scan the QR code below, enter your email and I'll send you all the files. Happy reading!

# Check out my other books!

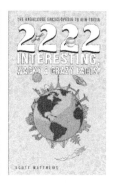

Printed in Great Britain
by Amazon

23578610R00086